ENJOYING

THE PRESENCE OF THE

LORD

EVERY DAY

ENJOYING
THE PRESENCE OF THE
LORD
EVERY DAY

Ernest J. Murat

Enjoying the Presence of the Lord Every Day

iUniverse books may be ordered through booksellers or by contacting:

iUniverse
1663 Liberty Drive
Bloomington, IN 47403
www.iuniverse.com
1-800-Authors (1-800-288-4677)

ISBN: 978-1-4917-8845-5 (sc)
ISBN: 978-1-4917-8846-2 (e)

Library of Congress Control Number: 2016901623

Print information available on the last page.

iUniverse rev. date: 02/27/2016

CONTENTS

INTRODUCTION

One day, as I was preparing to go into the field to complete a mission, I was simply enjoying the presence of the Lord, really bathing in His presence.

The Holy Spirit spoke to me concerning the book He wanted me to write. (This is the book you are now reading, the second book I have written.) He said, "Son, I want you to write a book about your experiences in My presence."

His urging was very strong; however, I had to complete the task at hand, which was to complete a two-week missionary trip to Dominican Republic. I was scheduled to depart in a month's time.

I knew that after I returned from the mission trip, I was to follow the demand of God: to write a book about how to enjoy the presence of the Lord every day. During those two weeks in Dominican Republic, I really meditated on just how potent and effective His presence is. In every meeting with Him, we experience the manifestation of His power. Each service is greater than the one before.

We at Worldwide Agape Ministry (WAM) also had an opportunity to experience His presence in a greater dimension, not only individually but also corporately during this mission trip. I will discuss this in greater detail later on (see chapter 2). For now, let's just say that He really showed Himself strong on our behalf during that trip. It was much more powerful than what we had experienced before. The intensity was greater, and the impact was more profound. Why? Why was the impact so profound, and why was the intensity so strong? God desires to perform a great awakening that's going to involve all of us. Within this great awakening, which is occurring right now through various ministries and churches, He is looking for willing vessels to receive His Spirit when He pours it out.

He is not looking for spectators; He is looking for participators. Those who do not mind getting involved will be blessed. It's going to take all of us to get involved. There is a great outpouring of the love of God that is going on right now. He is looking for people who are available, like you and me. Are you a willing vessel? He can, and will, use you—but only if you allow Him to do so. The scriptures tell us that we are His workmanship, or His handyman. Do you desire to be used by God? He really does want to use you.

The New King James Version (NKJV) of Ephesians 2:10 tells us:

> For we are His workmanship, created in Christ Jesus for good works, which God prepared beforehand or (before the foundation of the world) that we should walk before hand.

The same passage in the Amplified Bible (AB) puts it this way:

> For we are God's (own) handiwork (His workmanship), recreated in Christ Jesus, (born anew) that we may do those good works which God predestined (planned beforehand) for us (taking paths which He prepared ahead of time), that we should walk in them (living the good life which He prearrange and made ready for us to live).

When you remain in His presence, you can enjoy the good life that He set for us even before the foundation of the world. However, you won't benefit from His plan for you if you don't partake in His goodness. You do that by spending time in the presence of the Lord. It does benefit us when we are abiding in His presence; it's truly the only way to go.

You see, my brothers and sisters, once you truly experience His presence in your life, you will never, ever be the same. It changes your life forever.

Some of the many questions people ask in regard to this include the following:

How do I experience His presence?

Or, what must I do to experience His presence?

What is the reason for receiving His presence?

What do I do once I've received His presence?

All these questions have answers, which you will receive throughout the course of this book.

As you pursue this subject, you'll see that you should never be apart from the presence of the Lord. It is essential that every believer should experience His presence. If you have not yet experienced that, well, fasten your seat belt—you are going to have the ride (and time) of your life!

1

What Is the Presence of the Lord?

The New King James Version (NKJV) of Acts 3:19 tells us this about the presence of the Lord:

> Repent therefore and be converted, that your sins may be blotted out, so that times of refreshing shall come from the presence of the Lord.

Before we discuss what it is, let's talk about what it isn't. The presence of the Lord is not some scary, spooky feeling. It is not some dark cloud that comes out of the sky. It is not human reasoning, thoughts, ideas, or traditions. No human can duplicate it. It cannot be forced on people; it can only be obtained from God almighty. He is the original architect.

It is an original and authentic presence. The presence of God is not a human thing; rather, it is a God thing. It is God's super on our natural. It is fresh, revitalizing, renewing, and joyful. The above scripture truly describes it as refreshing. The first part of the scripture says to repent, to turn around and return to God.

His presence is about to invade your life. That means you must change your way of doing things.

Let's take a closer look at Acts 3:19. The Amplified Bible (AB) really clarifies the meaning of this verse:

> So repent (change your mind and purpose); turn around and return (to God), that your sins may be erased (blotted out, wiped clean), that time of refreshing (of recovering from the effects of heat, of reviving with fresh air) may come from the presence of the Lord.

The presence of God is supernatural. This is a truly amazing concept, to say the least. It is God's supernatural power pouring upon human flesh. It is God's power working on humans, enabling us to achieve greater results than we would be able to do on our own—that is, with our natural abilities and without his supernatural power.

The God of the universe—that awesome being who spoke the world into existence and can destroy mankind if He chooses to do so—makes His power accessible to each of us. Really? Divine power is obtainable and achievable? How?

Through Him. He has given you and me the opportunity to walk into His throne room, into fellowship with Him. Fellowship with God is truly a great experience. Any of His children can experience His throne room through fellowship with Him.

Yes, you can experience that thrilling and overwhelming joy simply by being in fellowship with Him. And, yes, you receive this great outpouring of joy just by spending time with God and fellowshipping with Him. Just as Adam and Eve did in the beginning, before sin occurred.

However, once they fell into sin, they no longer enjoyed close intimacy with Him. In fact, they were cast out of Eden, out of the presence of God. Sin causes everything to change. It was not that He did not know where Adam was; it was simply that the sin Adam and Eve committed changed the whole dynamic of their relationship with God.

Stay away from sin, and then you will experience the glory of God in a greater way. Keep sin out, and keep the presence in.

As we read in Genesis 3:8–10 out of the Amplified Bible (AB):

> And they heard the sound of the Lord God walking in the garden in the cool of the day, and Adam and his wife hid themselves from the presence of the Lord God among the trees of the garden.
>
> But the Lord God called to Adam and said to him, where are you?
>
> He said I heard the sound of you (walking) in the garden, and I was afraid because I was naked; I hid myself.

Look at what happened to Adam and Eve: Because of their disobedience, God stripped them of their covering of glory. Their sin also stripped them of their ability to stand in God's presence, with no sense of shame. That is truly the result of sin: it robs us of our confidence before God, because God absolutely hates sin.

Before falling into sin, do you believe that Adam and Eve greeted God's presence in the garden with fear, shame, or a sense of unworthiness? No, not all! They greeted Him with joy, happiness, and a total sense of belonging.

Sin is a presence blocker, and it is also a blessing blocker. This is one of the many reasons why God hates sin. Sin prevents God from getting near to the very creation that He loves and created in His own image: mankind. Yes, He does love you and me. God loves all His creation, but He loves us the most. Why? Because we have His breath in us.

The Amplified Bible (AB) of Genesis 2:7 tells us:

Then the Lord God formed man from the dust of the ground and breathed into his nostrils the breath or spirit of life, and man became a living soul.

We should always feel that we belong to Him. His presence is within us; however, we have to acknowledge Him. He still gives us the ability to choose. God will not override our will to choose Him or not choose Him. Although He prefers that we choose Him over everything and everyone, He loves us enough to allow each of us to choose. He loves us so much, it is beyond our understanding.

We really don't understand the magnitude of His love for us. If we did, we would not do some of the things we do. All of us have done some crazy things. God forgives us, but we each much choose to seek his forgiveness, another part of His presence.

As with forgiveness, His presence also brings love.

We see this in Romans 8:35 out of the New King James Version (NKJV):

Who shall separate us from the love of Christ? Shall tribulation, or distress, or persecution, or famine, or nakedness, or peril, or sword?

The answer is: No, not one of those things. Nothing can separate us from the love of God, and nothing can take His presence away from us. We may do a few things that may cause Him to draw back, to move away from us; but we only have to repent, and we will return to walking with Him and fellowshipping with Him, just as Adam and Eve did before they sinned.

We read this description of God's presence in Psalm 27:10, Common English Version (CEV):

Even if my father and mother should desert or abandon me, you will take care of me.

Here, the psalmist tells us that His presence is so strong that He will be with us, even if those who are supposed to be the closest to us abandon or desert us. He will still be there for us, no matter what. What an awesome God!

Confession

Repeat these truths as often as you need to:

> I have the presence of God within me. Everywhere I go, He is with me. The presence of God causes me to prosper; it causes me to be refreshed, joyful, peaceful, and loving. I have the love of God working within me.
>
> He causes me to triumph. His presence causes me to be an overcomer. I am an overcomer. I overcome Satan, by the blood of the Lamb and by the word of my testimony.
>
> In the mighty name of Jesus, amen.

2

WALKING WITH HIM, IN HIS PRESENCE

The New King James Version (NKJV) of Genesis 5:21–22, 5:24 tells us:

> Enoch lived sixty-five years, and begot Methuselah, after he begot Methuselah, Enoch walked with God three hundred years, and had sons and daughters.
>
> And Enoch walked with God; and he was not, for God took him.

This scripture really fascinates me, especially when I take the time to meditate on it. Enoch lived until he was 365 years old. He was already sixty-five when his eldest son, Methuselah, was born; he (Enoch) then lived another three hundred years, during which time he fathered more children. That Enoch was sixty-five when his first child was born is a miracle in and of itself! Enoch's firstborn, Methuselah, was the longest-living man ever. Clearly, Enoch lived in the presence of God. The miracles bestowed on him attest to this fact; it is not typical for a man to become a father for the first time at age sixty-five. Enoch had to know God very well because he walked with Him.

The point is, when you spend as much time with God as Enoch did, and for as long as he did, there is nothing God won't do for you.

It is not at all unusual for God to grant miracles to believers. In fact, it's the norm for Him. I believe Enoch's longevity and ability to father children at such an advanced age is an instance of God's intervention. Simply put, what seems impossible for men is absolutely possible for God!

As Mark 9:23 tells us: In the New King James Version (NKJV)

Jesus said, all things are possible to him who believes.

The other aspect of the scripture regarding Enoch that is even more impressive is that he walked (*in habitual fellowship*) with God for three hundred years. Enoch then disappeared from the earth in an unusual fashion. As we read in the above scripture: "And Enoch walked with God; and he was not, for God took him."

How did that happen? It happened to a man who knew how to fellowship with His Daddy. What fellowship that must have been!

The key issue here seems to be that Enoch continually walked, or fellowshipped, with God. He never let God go. He did not allow hard times to get the best of him. He did not allow his friends or loved ones to persuade him out of the presence of God. Enoch took the meaning of the word *faithful* to a new level.

Some of us start walking with God for just five minutes, and we are ready to give up. Enoch provides a great example of remaining steady at the feet of God, in fellowship with Him for as long as he lived. That is what lifelong faith is, even if we live for three hundred years.

Enoch was so much in tune with Daddy that he wanted to go home in a very special way. God honored that desire, allowing Enoch to simply disappear at the time He ordained. The scripture tells us that God just took Enoch. There was no funeral procession; there was no expensive casket to eventually decay underground; there was no viewing of the body or offering condolences to the bereaved family.

You've probably often asked some of the same questions that most people do when they read this story. How did this happen? How did Enoch manage to stay so long in God's presence, without any issues?

When I began to meditate on this, the Holy Spirit told me, "It was Enoch's choice. He knew how to enter into, abide within, and continually rest in My presence."

Most people cannot even fathom the thought of that, let alone do it.

Even though Enoch was the first man in history to be taken up to heaven without dying, he certainly will not be the last. I believe this kind of thing will occur more often in our lifetime. Why? Because it has been prophesied by many prominent, seasoned men of God. I heard one of these prominent men of God say that "this is a year of manifestation, visitation, and demonstration of the power of God." Many of the things that the prophets of old prophesied are coming to pass in our lifetime.

My brothers and sisters, you too can remain in Him. When you do abide in Him, whatever you desire, you shall receive; when you pray, believe that you receive it, and it shall come to pass.

As we read in John 15:7: In the New King James Version (NKJV)

> If you remain (abide) in me, and my words remain (abide) in you, you shall ask whatever you desire, and it shall be done for you.

My Own Testimony

Let me now tell you more about the mission trip I mentioned in the introduction. I met with the some of the pastors in fraternity churches in Santiago, Dominican Republic. This was just a simple meeting for us to get to know each other a bit, as I was going to minister in their churches.

I sensed the presence of God was among us, in a very strong way, but the meeting was not a formal one, just an icebreaker.

I asked the Holy Spirit, "What do You want me to do in this meeting? How do You want me to bless these brothers and sisters?"

He said, "I want you to share seven steps that they can take to help their ministries become successful."

I did exactly what the Holy Spirit told me to do. He had already put in my heart what He wanted me to share with them. The meeting turned out to be an explosive impartation from the Holy Ghost. It was an unforgettable experience.

Needless to say, the presence of God moves in very wonderful ways. I did not know what was happening in those churches, but the Holy Spirit knew. The Holy Spirit knows each one of us personally. He knows you better than you know yourself. He knew exactly what those pastors needed to hear. He moved through me to implement the improvements and changes He wanted to make. He always knows exactly what He wants.

We will explore the seven steps the Holy Spirit had me share with those pastors (see chapter 6). For now, it is sufficient to know that He seeks willing vessels. Do you remember what He said in the book of Isaiah? He is looking for a willing and obedient heart. Don't get too busy in your own personal affairs, or you will miss the instructions of the Holy Ghost.

This is what the King James Version (KJV) of Isaiah 1:19–20 tells us:

> If you are willing and obedient you shall eat the good of the land. But if you refuse and rebel, you shall be devoured with the sword: for the mouth of the Lord hath spoken it.

Here is the same verse in the New International Version (NIV):

> You shall eat the best of what the land has to offer.
>
> But if you refuse and rebel you shall be devoured with the sword: for the mouth of the Lord hath spoken it.

Confession

Repeat these truths as often as you need to:

> I decree and declare that I walk in His presence. I am an ambassador of Almighty God. His presence brings comfort to me. I have the joy of the Lord. The joy of the Lord is my strength. I am strong in the Lord and in the power of His might.
>
> I fellowship with Him; therefore, He strengthens me. His presence brings me wholeness and soundness, nothing missing and nothing broken.
>
> In the mighty name of Jesus, amen.

3

DRAWING IN:
HOW DO WE ENTER INTO
HIS PRESENCE?

James 4:8 tells us: In the New King James Version (NKJV)

Draw near to God and He will draw near to you.

It is very important to draw near to Him on a daily basis. Is it really that simple? Yes, indeed, it is. You must involve Him in your affairs in order to feel His presence in your life. Know that our God is a loving God. If you show him just a hint of your willingness to change, He will move heaven and earth to help you. He will work on your behalf to get you into His presence. In other words, you get into His presence by drawing near to Him every day.

You should come before Him before you leave your house every day, letting Him know that you are going to need Him that day, just as you do every day. Let Him know that you need Him to intervene in your affairs, and He will. He will show you what to do when you don't know what to do. Why? Because you are inviting Him into your affairs and into your life. You are opening the door to let Him in. What do you think will happen? He will come into your life and stay in your life; all you have to do is let Him in.

Once you begin to speak to Him on a regular basis, He will speak to you. He will tell you what will be discussed in the board meeting before the meeting actually takes place. You have an unseen partner working with you. How do you get this unseen partner? Again, just simply ask Him.

The Holy Spirit is a gentleman. He won't get involved in your affair unless you invite Him. He won't force Himself into your life, and He won't push His ways on you. He loves you enough to give you the ability to choose Him—or not choose Him.

When you invite Him in, you are guaranteeing your success. Why? Because you have given Him access to work on your behalf. As a result, you are destined to win every time. So why not get Him involved?

With Him as your partner, you have supernatural insight and knowledge working in your favor. Use these gifts to your advantage. He is available to you twenty-four hours a day, seven days a week. The presence of God is available to His children all the time, but because we don't fellowship with Him enough, we don't know that His word enough. We don't know what's available to us. And we don't incorporate faith into our daily lives.

As Hebrews 4:1–2 in the Amplified Bible (AB) tells us:

> Therefore, while the promise of entering His rest still holds and is offered (today), let us be afraid (to distrust it) lest any of you should think he has come too late and has come short of (reaching) it.
>
> For indeed we have had the glad tidings (gospel of God) proclaimed to us just as truly as they (the

Israelites of old did when the good news of deliverance from bondage came to them); but the message that they heard did not benefit them, because it was not mixed with faith (with the leaning of the entire personality on God in absolute trust and confidence in His power, wisdom, and goodness) by those who heard it; neither were they united in faith with the ones (Joshua and Caleb) who heard (did believe).

To put this differently, we have difficulty implementing what He gives us because we do not access it through faith. We can only receive what He offers us when we take it on faith and accept it with faith. According to His word, we receive all the promises that He has for us. However, we must apply faith to receive those promises.

The New King James Version (NKJV) of Romans 10:17 explains it this way:

So then faith comes by hearing, and hearing by the word of God.

The New King James Version (NKJV) of Hebrews 10:38 tells us succinctly:

The Just shall live by faith.

And Hebrews 11:6, from the New King James Version (NKJV), reinforces the importance of faith in our fellowship with God:

But without faith it is impossible to please Him. For He who comes to God must believe that He is, and that He is a rewarder of those who diligently seek God.

Therefore, the more time you spend with Him and His word, the more likely you will get to know Him, and then, the more likely you will receive what you expect from Him. Everything God has for us we must take and receive with and in faith. If you don't apply faith, you won't receive anything. We must live by faith.

He is a loving God. He truly wants to give you and me the very best. He is not trying to withhold anything from us. He just wants to make sure that we get all that He has available for us.

The New King James Version (NKJV) of Deuteronomy 29:29 tells us:

> The secret things belong to the Lord our God, but those things which are revealed belong to us and to our children forever; that we may do all the words of this law.

God wants to do great things for all His children. And all He wants in return is for us to acknowledge Him. Give Him back the glory that is His due. After all, it is He who causes us to prosper. He will do what He has said He will do. He stands firm on His promises, and so they all will surely come to pass.

As Isaiah 48:17–18 in the New King James Version (NKJV) tells us:

> Thus said the Lord, your redeemer, The Holy One of Israel:
>
> "I am the Lord your God, who teaches you to profit, who lead you in the way you should go.
>
> "Oh, that you had heeded my commandments! Then your peace would have been like a river, and your righteousness like the wave of the sea."

Here are the same verses of Isaiah in the Common English Version (CEV):

> By the power of his Spirit, the Lord God had sent me with this message: People of Israel, I am the Holy Lord God, the one who rescue you. For your own good, I teach you and lead you along the right path.
>
> How I wish that you had obeyed my commands! Your success and good fortune would have overflowed like a flooding river.

Yes, He truly does want to bless us and give us peace and restoration, but it all really depends on us. If we love Him, we will follow His commandments and make every effort to draw closer to Him. We first have to make whatever changes are necessary to do that, though. To put this in contemporary terms, God has given us access to download our blessings, but it's up to us to apply the faith we need in order to do it.

God always has our best interest at heart. However, He is a jealous God; He wants us to put Him first, and we should. Above all else, we should put God first. We must put Him before our spouses, before our children, before our parents, before anyone or anything dear to us. We must learn to put God first. It's in Him that we must trust. When we do, everything else will fall into its proper place.

As we read in Matthew 6:33 in the New King James Version (NKJV):

> Seek first the kingdom of God and His righteousness and all these things shall be added to you.

How much do you really trust Him? Remember, the more you seek Him, the more likely you are to experience His presence. We must desire to seek God first and to give Him first priority in our lives. Put Him first, before everything else and everyone else, and then He will work all things to your advantage. It is by putting God first, and by following His way of doing things, that all else will fall into its proper place.

My Own Testimony

Let me share another example from my own life. When I received my calling to the ministry, I was a twenty-two-year-old sailor in the United States Navy. I did not have much understanding of the Word of God; nor did I have a clear understanding of what was really happening in my life during that time. I went to church from time to time, but I was not at all serious in regard to the things of God.

Yet by the grace of God, my life was about to change forever. It was the prayers of my grandmother that caused God to move on my behalf during my younger years. Later on, it was my wife who interceded for me with God. Thank God for praying women! God has a special soft heart for women, especially those who like to come before His face all the time.

Most men are usually too busy with their own agendas to make time for God. Men usually don't like people to tell them what to do. Sometimes their agendas are complicated, sometimes not. A man's agenda might simply be a special sporting event. When you completely submit to God, however, nothing is more important than He is. For true believers, no sporting event is higher on the priority list than spending time in prayer with Daddy God. Don't misunderstand me: I enjoy all kinds of sports, just like the next guy; however, God is the top priority, first and always.

Back to my grandmother. She was the first prayer warrior I ever knew. When I was a little boy, she would pray all night long. I would lie asleep beside her, hearing her moaning and groaning throughout the night. I thought all grandmothers were like that. She prayed constantly, and she prophesied over me too, saying things like, "You are called." At the time, I really did not know what that meant. I do know today, though, and I thank God for her persistent prayers.

I lived with my grandmother from the time I was two years old until I was about five. She raised me during those tender years. Afterward, I moved with my mother from Haiti to the United States. It was a big change in my life, and it was not for the better. In fact, my life was no longer what it had been. I no longer attended church regularly. I grew into a lost and confused young man.

I loved to travel when I was young, and so I left college and joined the United States Navy. One year prior to leaving the navy, I met the love of my life (my wife, Jeanne). Jeanne was a missionary from Haiti, and we fell deeply in love. We married a year after we met. It was the best thing that ever happened to me.

Meeting Jeanne was the turning point of my life. She did not try to change me. She allowed the Holy Spirit to do that, one day at a time. She kept praying for me as I traveled with the navy. It does make a difference when you have someone interceding on your behalf. Regardless of what the situation looks in the natural, you (or your intercessor) must keep on praying. Circumstances will eventually change. In my case, the hedge of protection worked because of the prayers for me—first from my grandmother, and then from my wife. These God-fearing women constantly bombarded heaven on my behalf. The changes soon began to take place, one step at time. This was how I recognized my calling, as I mentioned earlier.

It happened while I was aboard a warship (which is like a city on water). At that time, it was a newly commissioned aircraft carrier. Even though I had not completely surrendered to God and did not yet walk with Him daily, I had a godly moment in my life. How is that even possible? By the grace of God, that's how!

That godly moment saved my life. I did not know it then, but I do know it now, with absolute, unequivocal faith. The grace of God kept me alive. It was quite beyond my comprehension at the time, but the hand of God was upon my life.

Here is what happened. After six months at sea, I was on duty during the midnight watch (12:00 a.m. to 4:00 a.m.), and I fell off the second deck of the ship (the aircraft carrier I mentioned previously). I was in the dirty, oily water for about two hours. I lost consciousness and nearly died. The enemy was attempting to cut my life short. But as I said, the grace of God kept me alive.

Thank God there were other watch standers (the officer of the day and other lookouts). They went down into the water immediately to rescue me. They took me to the sick bay (the clinic inside the ship). The duty corpsman (a medic who serves as a nurse) called the ship's doctor to examine me.

While I was lying in the sick bay, I saw my spirit leave my body. And then I heard my grandmother's voice speak to me, saying, "You will not die. You shall live to fulfill your call: to preach the gospel all over the world. You have not yet fulfilled the plan of God in your life." I believe now that this was an angel taking the form of my grandmother; I recognized both her voice and her face.

Immediately after hearing those words, my spirit went back into my body. I was awake. Everyone in the room was very shocked to see my eyes open, because moments before I was not able to breathe at all. God had resurrected me. I will say it again: I am alive today by the grace of God.

Glory to God, who lives forevermore. What the enemy intended for bad, God turned around for His good. Today, I am a traveling missionary serving the Almighty. I am ready and willing to preach and teach the gospel (the good news) wherever and whenever He sends me. And whenever a door is opened through Him, I respond by saying, "Sir, yes, sir! Whatever you say, sir!"

Confession

Repeat these truths as often as you need to:

> I am what the Word of God says I am. I can have what the Word of God says I can have. I can do what the Word of God says I can do. I can be what the Word of God says I can be. I am a new creation, born again in Christ Jesus. I am the righteousness of God in Christ Jesus. I have the faith of God residing within me.
>
> I can do all things through Christ who strengthens me. I can minister with God's ability. I can always triumph in Christ Jesus.
>
> I live constantly in the presence of God. The Lord will keep me from all harm. He will watch over my life. The Lord will watch over my coming in and my going out, both now and forevermore.
>
> In the mighty name of Jesus, amen.

4

SHOW ME YOUR GLORY!

Exodus 33:11–15 tells us in the New King James Version (NKJV):

> So the Lord spoke to Moses face to face, as a man speak to his friend. And he would return to the camp, but his servant Joshua son of Nun, a young man, did not depart from the tabernacle.
>
> Then Moses said to the Lord, "See, you say to me, 'Bring up this people.' But you have not let me know whom you will send with me. Yet you have said, 'I know you by name, and I also find grace in my sight.'"
>
> "Now therefore, I pray, if I have found grace in your sight, show me now your way, that I may know you and that I may find grace in your sight. And consider that this nation is your people."
>
> And He said, "My presence would go with you, and I will give you rest."
>
> Then he said to Him, "If your presence does not go with us, do not bring us up from here."

This is a great communication between Moses and God. It is like two best friends talking to each other. The exchange is awesome. God basically tells Moses, "My presence will be with you; and by the way, I will also give you rest."

Moses then tells God, "Yes, sir, because if Your presence is not there, I don't want to go there, either."

Moses understood something about the presence of God that most believers today don't understand. He recognized that it was the presence of God that would carry him all the way through to the Promised Land. If you do not have that understanding, you do not have anything going for you.

Moses had the wisdom to know that abiding in the presence of God would give him the power and provision to make it through. You have to know that having the presence of God in your life is very essential, even today—especially today.

When you abide in His presence, there is nothing that you will lack. Whatever you need will be provided in His presence. What is it that you need today? You can receive it as soon as you come into His presence. His presence means that nothing is missing and nothing is broken. Nothing is too far-fetched, and nothing is unachievable or unattainable.

Take a thirty-second praise break, and get into His presence right now.

Get Hungry for His Presence

Moses was hungry for His presence; in fact, he wanted even more. What he is saying to God in the above scripture, in essence, is that he wanted an abundance of God's presence. "Don't just give me a little dabs here and there, Lord. I want much, much more."

That is the kind of attitude God requires of us, and He desires to give to us abundantly. However, we must have a hunger and thirst for His presence. Desire Him more and more, because He desires to do great things in your life, but you must put a demand on it. The anointing is neither free nor cheap. It is very costly. Let Him know that you will keep seeking Him until you feel His presence.

God has a plan and a purpose for us. We must stay hungry in order to accomplish the task He sets before us. We must have that strong desire to fulfill God's plan and purpose for us. When we do, there is nothing that the enemy can steal from us.

God will use you when you are hungry for Him. He desires to pour out His love, His anointing, and His divine glory to whomever He so desires. He is simply looking for empty vessels, ready vessels that are hungry to seek and know Him. It does not matter what it takes; if He chooses you, He'll use you.

He is not looking for the smartest guy in town; nor is He looking for the guy who thinks nobody can tell him what to do. Why? Because the pride of such people gets in the way. God is looking for people who are available, first and foremost, and who are flexible, teachable, and willing to go the extra mile when required. If you are set in your ways, unbending and unwilling, then no one can use you. You are of no use to anyone, including yourself. God knows this.

Moreover, staying hungry keeps you flexible, teachable, and willing. God knows this too, and He reveals it through Moses.

In Exodus 33:18, we read in the New King James Version (NKJV):

And he said, "Please, show me your glory!"

Staying hungry, Moses was no longer satisfied to fellowship with God from the middle of a dense cloud. After he had experienced a little of God's glorious presence, he wanted more!

What he's really saying here is, "Give me much, much more! Get this cloud of my way; I want to see your glory! Lord, I want to see your face!"

God loves that, even though He knows what you are and aren't capable of handling. God did not say no to Moses. God will always grant you fellowship and revelation to whatever degree you can handle without being harmed.

Basically, God's response to Moses is, "Okay. If that's you want, then that's what you'll get. Here it is: wham!"

Thus, Exodus 33:19–23 states in the New King James Version (NKJV):

> Then He said, "I will make all My goodness pass before you, and I will proclaim the name of the Lord before you, I will be gracious to whom I will be gracious, and I will have compassion on whom I will have compassion."
>
> But He said, "You cannot see my face; for no man shall see Me, and live,"
>
> And the Lord said, "Here is a place by Me, and you shall stand on a rock,
>
> So it shall be, while My glory passes by, that I will put you in the cleft of the rock, and will cover you with My hand while I pass by.
>
> Then I will take away My hand, and you shall see My back; but My face shall not be seen."

Wow! This is a powerful exchange between God and Moses. Through these verses, He shows us that even though He is the Master and Creator of the universe, we each can still fellowship and communicate with Him. And He lets each of that do that on different levels, whichever level is right for us. The above verses describe the highest level any man had ever fellowshipped with God (up to that point), without damaging himself. It was a great accomplishment for Moses. Although it was a great accomplishment, it was still at a limited level, foreshadowing the fellowship that would come with Jesus. The cleft in the rock is a further foreshadowing of Jesus, the ultimate Rock in the New King James Version (NKJV) of 1 Cor. 10:4. It is in Him that we are able to experience God's goodness and glory.

The glory does not end there. We can still experience the glory of God today. In the second chapter of the book of Acts, we read about how the earlier church experienced the glory in the form of the sound of a rushing mighty wind that filled the entire house where they were sitting. The glory is still available today. The way you receive it depends completely on you. How hungry are you?

When we refer to "the glory," what are we really talking about? The fire of God is also called the glory of God. The wind of God also refers to the glory. The smoke and the fullness of God are the glory of God.

He wants us to go deeper in our walk with Him. He wants us to develop a deeper relationship with Him. He is not looking for a lukewarm or shallow relationship. He pretty much said, "If you are lukewarm, I'll spit you out." He wants us to know there is much, much more available us—for you and for me. Let's go deeper; let's confront His presence as if it's the last time we are going to see Him or be with Him. There is so much He wants to do for us, but unless we put enough effort into receiving what He has available for us, and unless we accept it in faith, we will get nothing.

As Psalm 41:7 tells us in the New King James Version (NKJV):

Deep calls unto deep at the noise of Your waterfalls.
All Your waves and billows have gone over me.

Confession

Repeat these truths as often as you need to:

> I decree and declare that I experience the glory of God. I experience the love of God, and I experience the fullness of God. The Love of God is abiding in me, richly.
>
> He has given me richly all things to enjoy. He is my Jehovah Jireh. He is my provider. My God shall supply all my needs, according to His riches and glory, through Christ Jesus.
>
> In the mighty name of Jesus, amen.

5

MANIFESTING GLORY
FOR TODAY

A contemporary translation of the Bible, The Message (MSG), phrases Acts 2:1 this way:

> When the Feast of Pentecost came, they were all together in one place. Without warning was a sound like a strong wind, gale force—no one can tell where it came from. It filled the whole building. Then, like a wildfire, the Holy Spirit spread through their ranks, and they started speaking in a number of different languages as the Spirit prompted them.

This is the glory of God, as manifested in the New Testament. It was—and is—the power of God that is described in the above passage. That same great power that occurred on the day of Pentecost is still here today. It is the Spirit of almighty God, and He is still available to abide within each of us forever.

In the Old Testament, the Spirit of God was only available for a specific task or purpose. The Spirit came upon the prophets when needed to fulfill God's purpose, but it did not remain within each of them. But now, through Christ Jesus, the Spirit of God is available for everyone who seeks Him, who hungers for Him. Also, because of Jesus, the Spirit is within us (indwelling), not upon us.

You could be supercharging on the Spirit right now, regardless of who you are and where you are, regardless of the color of your skin and what you do to earn a living. The Spirit of God is not biased. He is simply looking for hungry and available hearts.

You can experience the glory of God today, just like the brothers and sisters did centuries ago at the Feast of the Pentecost. You just have to be hungry. Start developing a spirit of hunger, showing you desire the power of God to manifest in your life. Once the glory of God starts to manifest in your life, you will never be the same.

Start fellowshipping with God and chewing on His word daily. Your relationship with Him will grow tremendously. Get into His word; start meditating on His word. We've already talked a bit about meditating on His word. Simply put, it means that you shouldn't just read His word; you should also study His word, and after you study it, you should think about what you just read. Ponder on it as much as you need to. You should also confess His word. Let it bubble up inside of you. Let His word speak to you.

As we read in Joshua 1:8 in the Amplified Bible (AB):

This book of the law shall not depart from your mouth, but you shall meditate on it day and night, you may observe and do according to all that is written in it. For then you shall make your way prosperous, and then you shall deal wisely and have good success.

This is what meditation does. It takes you to a newer realm with Daddy God. This realm is as yet unknown to you, but it is well known to God. It is the realm of the supernatural. He wants to take you there.

Once you really meditate on His word, you will go to a place far deeper, and far higher, spiritually. Start meditating on His word and His goodness. You will begin to see the changes in your life. You will see the progress you have made. You will be surprised by what He will do for you. God is good, and His mercy endureth forever.

His Goodness and Mercy Manifest in Our Lives

In Psalm 16:11 in the New King James Version (NKJV), we read:

> You will show me the path of life; In Your presence there is fullness of joy; At Your right hand are pleasures forever more.

His goodness shows us the way. When you get into His presence, He will lead you, guide you, and direct you. He will show you what to do and which path to take in life. God is interested in your personal life. He will show you the right person to marry. He will let you know what to do concerning those big decisions that come up in life. He will always be there, with you and for you. He will lead you on the right path. All you have to do is get Him involved in your life. All these things require His presence; He can't do them for you if you don't let him into your life. The fullness of joy comes from His presence.

One man who had a great revelation of this truth was David. David wrote Psalm 51 after he admitted committing adultery with Bathsheba; he was remorseful when the prophet confronted him about his sin. He knew that he only had one option: to get into the presence of God, for that alone produces the fullness of joy.

In the New King James Version (NKJV), Psalm 51:7–11 tells us:

> Purge me with hyssop, and I shall be clean; Wash me, and I shall be whiter than snow.
>
> Make me hear joy of gladness that the bones you have broken may rejoice.
>
> Hide your face from my sins, And blot out all my iniquities.
>
> Create in me a clean heart, O God, And renew a steadfast spirit within me.
>
> Do not cast me away from your presence, And do not take your Holy Spirit away from me

David clearly understood that without the presence of God, you are nothing. You can't do anything right. David was adamant about this because he experienced both the presence and absence of God. It is not fun to be out of the presence of God.

When you are out of His presence, you are dry. You are not only dry spiritually, but emotionally you are a nervous wreck, unable to control yourself. Everything you do seems to be one disaster after another. This is only because you need a dose of His heavenly presence, just His breath to waft over you and into you. (In the next chapter, we will explore how to get Him to do that.) Let Him breathe in you. Get into His word. Start praying in the Spirit. If you don't how, ask Him. Praying in the Spirit is a gift—His gift to each of us, and you can have it. But you have to ask!

If you are not saved, get saved. This is the only way you will receive the total package we've been talking about. At the end of this book, you will find a prayer titled "Prayer for Salvation and Baptism in the Holy Spirit." Use this prayer to ask Jesus to come into your life. Don't miss out on the opportunity that Jesus has for you. The glory can begin to manifest in your life today.

Confession

Repeat these truths as often as you need to:

> I decree and declare this is the best year of my life. I experience the greater glory. I experience God's manifestation, His visitation, and His demonstration, today. His presence has made me an overcomer. I overcome sin, sickness, demons, fear, depression, oppression, lack, poverty, debt, and any other things that the enemy tries to throw at me. I rebuke it all, in the mighty name of Jesus.
>
> I decree and declare that God's word is manifest in my life. He is the way, the truth, and the life. He is the greater one. He resides in me. Greater is He that is in me than he that is in the world. I believe I receive everything that I ask for.
>
> In the mighty name of Jesus, amen.

6

ENTER INTO HIS PRESENCE

As we read in the New King James Version (NKJV) of Psalm 63:1–8:

> O God, You are my God; Early will I seek You; My soul thirsts for You; My flesh longs for You in a dry and thirsty land where there is no water.
>
> So I have looked for you in the sanctuary, to see Your power and Your glory.
>
> Because Your loving kindness is better than life, My lips shall praise You.
>
> Thus I will bless You while I live; I will lift up my hands in Your name.
>
> My soul shall be satisfied as with marrow and fatness, And my mouth shall praise You with joyful lips.
>
> When I remember You in my bed, I meditate on You in the night watches.
>
> Because You have been my help, therefore in the shadow of Your wings I will rejoice.
>
> My soul follows close behind You; Your right hands uphold me.

The above verses show that you enter into His presence by doing several things, one of the most important of which is to praise Him. Praising God is one of the many ways to enter into His presence. When you praise Him, you begin to break the hollow ground. Satan hates believers who always praise God. By praising God, you make Satan weak; you strip him of his evil power, and he loses his strength.

A praising saint is a powerful saint. Let's take a thirty-second break to praise Him right now.

Another important thing that will get you into His presence is having a heart of gratitude and thanksgiving. When you are thankful for what He has done for you, show Him your gratitude. You are literally getting ready to open the windows of heaven. When you thank God for everything, you are inviting Him into your life.

In the New King James Version (NKJV), Philippians 4:6 puts it this way:

> Be anxious for nothing, but in everything by prayer and supplication, with thanksgiving, let your request be made known to God.

My Own Testimony

One afternoon, I got off work and headed for the highway to drive home. All of a sudden, I felt it was necessary to thank God. While I was driving on the highway, I begin to thank Him, including everything that I could think of at the time.

The presence of God was so thick in the car, I had to pull over for a few minutes. I sat in the car and just absorbed the presence of God that was manifest around me in a very strong and unexplainable way.

You see, my brothers and sisters, this is the kind of God we serve. He is always available for us. Do not take His glory (what belongs to Him)! Whenever He does something wonderful for you, thank Him.

As 1 Thessalonians 5:16, 18 tells us in the New King James Version (NKJV):

Rejoice always.

In everything, give thanks; for this is the will of God in Christ Jesus for you.

He always does great things for us, so we should have a heart of gratitude at all times. There is always a reason to thank Him. Bring Him on the scene. Why don't you do that right now? Take another thirty-second break. Thank Him right now. Hallelujah!

Give Him All the Glory

As we read in Psalm 103:1–2 in the New King James Version:

Bless the Lord, O my soul; And all that is within me, bless His holy name!

Bless the Lord, O my soul; And forget not all His benefits.

When you thank God for all His blessings and help, He will bless you even more, because you are accessing your blessing. Do not ever forget what He has done for you. You can brag about God's goodness. Tell as many people as you can about His goodness. As a matter of fact, He does not mind at all. Give Him all the glory that belongs to Him.

He loves when we give Him attention. Be aware that you are going to have some haters once God begins to bless you. Haters will come out of the woodwork, hating you for no reason. Do not let that bother you. You just keep on doing what God calls you to do. God will take care of you; just do what you are supposed to do.

Seven Steps to Success in the Spirit

Let's explore in detail the seven steps that the Holy Spirit imparted to me prior to my mission trip in Santiago, Dominican Republic, described briefly in chapter 2. You'll remember that the Holy Spirit told me to share these truths with the men of God I was about to meet with. In fact, while I was whispering my thanks to Him prior to that meeting, He gave me the truths to share. And then, while I worked on this book, He told me to share these truths with you as well.

So here, from the Holy Spirit, are seven steps to help you succeed in your business, in your day-to-day life, in your ministry or your church, and in all your activities and endeavors:

1. **Give God first priority in your business or ministry.** This includes your personal life. Put Him first, before anything else and anyone else.

2. **Be prayerful.** Always submit your calling in prayer, asking God what direction you should take. Through prayer, you will receive His answer, and then you will know what to do and how to do it.

3. **Be faithful and steadfast.** Your calling should always be before you: in your face, so to speak. Where do you want to go? Whatever He puts before you, accept

it; whatever He tells you to do right now, do it to the best of your ability.

4. **Love your ministry, and be passionate about it.** You will always have a passion for the things you love to do. Take it one small step at a time.

5. **Always fill yourself up.** Feed yourself as much as possible. Be ready, at a moment's notice, to seize every opportunity He grants you.

6. **Be teachable and flexible.** Maintain an excellent spirit and a can-do attitude. Always be open to learn more.

7. **You must love your product.** Our product is the Word of God. Whatever your product is, you must have a passion for it. You must know it like a craftsman knows and uses his tools. Love your product, and know your product very well.

Confession

Repeat these truths as often as you need to:

I decree and declare that I enter into His presence. It is in Him that I move and have my being. I am the righteousness of God. I am His workmanship.

Therefore, I am blessed; I am also blessed because I am a praiser. Because I am a praiser, I know how to thank Him.

I praise You and I thank You, Lord. You are my Daddy, and I love You.

In the mighty name of Jesus, amen.

7

WORSHIP HIM IN
DIFFERENT WAYS

We read in the New King James Version (NKJV) Ephesians
5:18–20:

> And do not be drunk with wine, in which is dissipation;
> but be filled with the Spirit
>
> Speaking to one another in psalms and hymns and
> spiritual songs, singing and making melody in your
> heart to the Lord,
>
> Giving thanks always for all things to God the
> Father in the name of our Lord Jesus Christ.

Worship is another key action to bring the presence of the
Lord into your life. If you ever desire to have Him closer to you,
then you must keep a heart of worship. You can sing songs that
bring glory and honor to Him. Not every song brings glory to
God, but songs of melody and adoration do. God loves when
His children worship Him through different means.

Nothing brings the presence of God more gloriously into
your life than the worship of Him through reciting psalms and
singing hymns and spiritual songs, both known and unknown.
You can make up your own songs to praise Him. Just have an

open heart when you present your words to Him. Present your gift, and adore Him with it.

It really does not matter how you worship God. He only cares that you *do* worship Him. He desires that you do it consistently and as often as possible.

My Own Testimony

A few years ago, the Holy Spirit asked my wife to worship Him every day. "Do not ask me for anything, just simply worship Me," He said.

Jeanne did what He told her to do, and she still does, to this very day. She still sets aside a specific time to be alone with God every day.

Remember, God is always looking for our availability. Are you available? If you are, He wants to use you. And the end result is always excellent.

God uses Jeanne in a very special way. I hardly ever go to preach without having her there. Because she is a worshipper, she helps to bring the glory of God to manifest in the place where we are. Jeanne and I work as a team. My anointing is amplified when we work together in harmony.

So start to worship Him, but do so without any hidden agenda. You will see the difference immediately. Our God is good, and His love and His mercy endure forever. He will bless you if you don't have an alternative agenda.

Instruments of Praise

In the New King James Version (NKJV), Psalm 150 tells us:

> Praise the Lord! Praise God in His sanctuary; Praise Him in His mighty firmament! Praise Him for His mighty acts; Praise Him according to His excellent greatness! Praise Him with sound of the trumpet, Praise Him with the lute and harp! Praise Him with the timbrel and dance; Praise Him with stringed instruments and flutes! Praise Him with loud cymbals! Let everything that has breath praise the Lord. Praise the Lord!

Psalm 150 tells us that we can use different kinds of instruments to praise and worship the Lord. God does not really care about what kind of instrument we use to honor Him; after all, He made each and every one of them.

Special Gifts Given by God

As 1 Corinthians 12:4–7 states in the New King James Version (NKJV):

> There are diversities of gifts, but the same Spirit. There are differences of ministries, but the same Lord. And there are diversities of activities, but it is the same God who works all in all. But the manifestation of the Spirit is given to each one for the profit of *all.*

All the gifts that God has given us are to edify the body and equip it to become a higher place of worship. God has given my wife and me a special gift that ushers in the presence of God: blowing the shofar (ram's horn). Jeanne and I blow the shofar at certain places and on certain occasions. Whenever we blow the shofar, at any service, the presence of God manifests. It is a special gift. We only blow the shofar under the leading of the Holy Spirit, but we do blow it in different places, as He directs us to do.

For instance, when Jeanne and I were in Haiti as missionaries, we stayed at a family member's house. It was a three-story home. One night, we felt that there were some strange activities happening in the spirit realm: demonic activities taking place in the neighborhood. We did not see anything in the natural realm, but there was something going on in the unseen realm. Therefore, we were led by the Holy Spirit to blow the shofar.

In the Old Testament, the priests used the shofar for a variety of rituals. The usage depended on the circumstances and the situation, but the shofar was used for various tasks. The shofar produces some very mystical sounds, which have some very unusual properties. One of its properties is the ability to stir a heart to repentance.

The shofar sounds similar to a trumpet, but its power is far greater. God used it destroy the walls of Jericho. The shofar is also used to get rid of demonic spirits or activities. The shofar brings peace. Certain sounds of the shofar bring the faithful together. The shofar represents the voice of God. It is still used today, under the guidance of the Holy Ghost.

According to the Talmud (sacred Jewish text), the shofar can be made of the horns of various animals, including both domestic and wild goats, the antelope, the gazelle, and, of course, the ram. (In Jewish synagogues, the shofar is still blown during the High Holy Days.)

The horn of a ram is most typically used, and it is preferred, as the shofar is strongly linked with the story of Abraham binding Isaac to sacrifice to HaShem (God). As we all know, an angel stopped Abraham, and HaShem provided a ram in Isaac's place.

Now, while a ram's horn is preferred, a cow's horn is forbidden. The Hakhamim (Pharisees) believed that if a cow's horn was used, it would give Satan the opportunity to continue to accuse Israel for the incident surrounding the golden calf, and then HaShem would be biased in His dealing with Israel. We believers know that our God is not a biased God. This is Old Testament thinking.

In the next chapter, we will explore the shofar in greater detail, illustrating the ways in which it brings the presence of God.

Confession

Repeat these truths as often as you need to:

I decree and declare I take charge of this atmosphere in this place. I plead the blood of Jesus over this place.

I worship God, in the presence of His holiness.

Holy Spirit, I welcome You in; have Your way in this place.

I worship You. You are my God. I love You. You are the best, Daddy. You are awesome. I give You first place. I can't do anything without You. I need You today. Have Your way in me.

Thank You, Daddy. I love You, Daddy.

In the mighty name of Jesus, amen.

8

THE MINISTRY OF THE SHOFAR BRINGS THE PRESENCE OF GOD

What Is the Shofar?

In the New King James Version (NKJV), Numbers 10:1–3, 8 describes the shofar this way:

> And the LORD spoke to Moses, saying: "Make two silver trumpets for yourself; you shall make them of hammered work; you shall use them for calling the congregation and for directing the movement of the camps. When they blow both of them, all the congregation shall gather before you at the door of the tabernacle of meeting.
>
> The sons of Aaron, the priests, shall blow the trumpets; and these shall be to you as an ordinance forever throughout your generations.

When scripture refers to the trumpet, it is the same as the shofar. Along with the harp, the shofar is the most frequently mentioned musical instrument in the Bible, yet most New Testament believers today don't know a thing about it.

Although widely used in biblical times, the harp is vastly different from the shofar. The harp is used to calm and soothe the spirit and soul, whereas the shofar is consistently used to grab hold of the attention and spirit of the people. However, the harp can also be used to bring the presence of God on the scene.

It is interesting to note that shofar can also be written as *shophar*. It is a Hebrew word whose root meaning is "beauty." Through tradition, however, the word *shofar* has come to mean "ram's horn" almost exclusively.

My Own Testimony

As mentioned previously, the shofar is an instrument that the Lord uses to touch the lives of hundreds, possibly thousands of people. The first time I used the instrument was in a dream. In the dream, I saw a man blowing a strange instrument.

I asked the Holy Spirit, "What is that strange-looking instrument that man is blowing?"

"The instrument is the shofar, and the man is you, my son," He said.

I had not realized that I was the man in my dream, and I had never seen a shofar before.

The Holy Spirit also said, "Use the shofar as your weapon; use it against the work the enemy."

I thought about what the Holy Spirit had told me concerning the shofar. I had a sort of sketch in my brain of the instrument I had seen in my dream. I wondered how I was to use a thirty-two-inch instrument to combat the work of the enemy. The shofar did not sound too impressive to me at the time. Since all this was new to me, I did not even know where to start. I kept meditating on it, and I also did some research on the Internet.

The following month, Jeanne and I went to a conference where Dr. Myles Munroe was the guest speaker, and we saw a couple blowing the shofar. It was a confirmation of what we were supposed to be doing. Today, we both blow the shofar, wherever the Holy Spirit leads us.

The Holy Spirit led Jeanne and me to blow the shofar on the top of a building in Haiti. We did what the Holy Spirit instructed us to do, and as I've said, we only blow the shofar under His guidance.

We blew the shofar twenty-one times that day, and all the demonic activities ceased afterward (this refers to the situation described in chapter 7). After we blew the shofar, there was a supernatural peace that only the presence of God can manifest. There was heavenly peace in the area.

Over the years, Jeanne and I have blown the shofar in various places and for various occasions: marriages, funeral services, businesses, prayer groups, personal homes, mountains, parks, and our own neighborhood. Why? Because the sounding of the shofar is the presence of God. It's the manifestation of His glory, the manifestation of His power, and the manifestation of His goodness. And all these are also known as the glory.

Wherever we go, people want to experience the presence of God. We are His vessels, and we submit to Him. The gift of blowing the shofar is from Him. No matter what your gifts are, you have to simply submit them to God. Remember, He gave them to you in the first place! All gifts are through Him.

Jeanne and I have traveled to various countries, and we always bring our shofars with us. Many people have asked us to blow the shofar in their homes. They've also often asked us to blow the shofar in specific ordination ceremonies, desiring the presence and power of God to move supernaturally through the ceremony. Today, we still blow the shofar, and will continue to do so for as long the Holy Spirit directs us.

The sound of the shofar is bold and pure; it calls the faithful. It summons the presence of God. The presence of God brings boldness, it brings restoration, and it brings deliverance. It also brings a breakthrough for any need you might have.

Experiencing the presence leads to experiencing the glory, which we will discuss in the next chapter.

Confession

Repeat these truths as often as you need to:

I decree and declare that I worship God. I worship Him in various forms. My God shall supply for all my needs, through Christ Jesus, according to His riches and glory. I am the righteousness of God. I praise my God with my shofar, and I bring glory to Him

It's in Him that I live and have my being. His presence is in me. The greater one resides in me. Therefore, I am what He says I am. I can have what He says I can have, and I can do what He says I can do. He is the hope and the glory.

In the mighty name of Jesus, amen.

9

EXPERIENCE THE GLORY

The New King James Version (NKJV) of Haggai 2:6–9 tells us this about the glory of God:

> "For thus says the Lord of hosts: 'Once more (it is a little while) I will shake heaven and earth, the sea and dry land; and I will shake all nations, and they shall come to the Desire of All Nations, and I will fill this temple with glory,' says the Lord of hosts. 'The silver is Mine, and the gold is Mine,' says the Lord of hosts. 'The glory of this latter temple shall be greater than the former,' says the Lord of hosts. 'And in this place I will give peace,' says the Lord of hosts."

We have already talked about the glory of God in general terms, but we really did not go into great detail. In this chapter, we will explore the glory further. Before we can do that, we must discuss the key aspects of God's glory.

The glory of God refers to these three key aspects:

1. manifestation of the presence of God
2. manifestation of the power of God
3. manifestation of the goodness of God

The above scripture tells us that the glory of God shall be greater in later times than in former times. This means that the greater glory which will manifest on earth is nigh; the time that the prophets of old have spoken about is here.

We can also discern from the above verses that we will experience the glory of God in a greater way. It will be sporadic at first—just here and there, so to speak—but then, it shall be manifest everywhere, and much greater than ever before.

It is also important to point out that the turmoil on earth keeps getting worse and worse. The repercussions will be even greater for people who don't have a relationship with Jesus. It is so vitally important to have a relationship with Jesus. (Again, "Prayer for Salvation and Baptism in the Holy Spirit," which appears at the end of this book, will show you how.)

We can rest assured that cursing Satan is also working. The enemy knows that his end is near. Therefore, he is turning on his engine full throttle here on earth, wreaking serious havoc with God's creation. The only certainty that we have to stop the work of the enemy is Jesus.

As Galatians 3:13 tells us in the New King James Version (NKJV):

> Christ has redeemed us from the curse of the law, having become a curse for us.

What about Our Current Time?

There has been a lot of speculation about our current time. Here are some prophecies from a few well-known men of God:

On October 18, 2014, Dr. Jerry Savelle declared, "This is the year of visitation, manifestations, and demonstrations of power of God!"

Let's emphasize that this prophecy will not come to pass automatically. We must reinforce it by demanding that it come to pass, and then it shall come to pass. We must each make a continuous confession until the desired result manifests.

When I hear words like the above prophecy, I receive with faith that such events come to pass in my life and in the lives of all believers. I confess these words as often as possible. Yes, the visitation, the manifestation, and the demonstration will come to pass in my life—and in yours too. They will come to pass in greater ways than ever before.

If you can stand in faith and believe this prophecy, as I do, then you can also experience the glory of God in greater measure. And let's remember that it does not have to happen in one particular year. Dr. Savelle said that "this is the year," but that does not necessarily refer to a specific year; it could also mean that it will happen in the years to come.

Bishop Keith Butler said, "God has given us an opportunity right now. Right now, the door is open. Opportunity for the Church to run through …"

Kenneth Copeland stated, "The word of the Lord came to me, saying, '*Twenty-fifteen is the year of the overcomer*! We will walk in the greatest supernatural victories of the overcoming faith which we have ever seen or heard.'"

All the above prophecies have come to us from God, as spoken through the great men He chose to speak for Him. What will happen in this season? Only God knows for sure. You may wonder how we can know that these prophecies are true. First, we must compare them with the scriptures. Next, we must judge them later on, based on whether or not they came to pass.

Regardless, we must remember that these men of God have spent countless hours before the Lord, listening to what

He has in store for us in every season. God speaks to them and through them on our behalf. God can also speak to you too. He is not limited. He speaks to these men for the body of Christ as whole. Look at the scripture below, and see how He does it. He is just that kind of God. He may speak to us if He so desires. He calls the shots. He does not need permission from anyone.

As Amos 3:7 tells us in the New King James Version (NKJV):

Surely the Lord God does nothing, unless He reveals His secret to His servants the prophets.

And as Romans 3:4 declares in the King James Version (KJV):

God forbid: yea, let God be true, but every man a liar; as it is written, That thou mightest be justified in thy sayings, and mightest overcome when thou art judged."

How Do I Receive the Glory in My Life?

Here are five steps to receive the glory and see it manifest in your life:

1. Keep a hungry and a thirsty heart for the things of God.

2. Be ready to change at a moment's notice, following God's word.

3. Have an open spirit, and an open heart, ready to do whatever He tells you to do. Whatever He tells you to do, just do it.

4. Pray in the Spirit a lot. Ask the Holy Spirit for interpretation.

5. Believe you receive it, and take it on faith. And then, thank Him for it.

What If It Does Not Work the First Time?

Well, keep doing it over and over, until it comes to pass. You must be willing to stand on God's word. No matter what it takes. Don't be fooled by the enemy.

God's word works, if you work it by faith. Repeat steps 1 through 5, above, as many times as necessary until the desired result manifests.

As we read in Galatians 5:9 in the New King James Version (NKJV):

And let us not grow weary while doing good, for in due season we shall reap if we do not lose heart.

The book of Isaiah discusses this too.

Isaiah 40:29 tells us in the New King James Version (NKJV):

He gives power to the weak, And to those who have no might He increases strength.

And In the New King James Version (NKJV), Isaiah 49:26 tells us:

"I will feed those who oppressed you with their own flesh, and they shall be drunk with their own blood as with a sweet wine. All flesh shall know. That I, the Lord, Am your Savior, and your Redeemer, the Mighty One of Jacob."

Do not let the enemy deceive you! God's word shall surely come to pass. He is your God, and surely He shall see you through. His greater glory will manifest in your life. And remember, His glory is the manifestation of His presence, His power, and His goodness. The greatest part of His goodness is His love, which we will discuss in the next chapter.

Confession

Repeat these truths as often as you need to:

> I decree and declare that the manifestation of His power shall manifest in my life. Supernatural provision shall also follow. Yes, this year is the best year of my life. This is a year when the unusual shall be usual for me. Those who hate to see progress in my life will have no choice but to call me *blessed.*
>
> I have the anointing of God in me. The blessing of the Lord brings wealth to me, without my having to toil for it painfully. I have the superabundant manifestation of God working within me and for me.
>
> In the mighty name of Jesus, amen.

10

BECAUSE OF HIS AGAPE: THE UNCONDITIONAL LOVE OF GOD

We read this in 1 Corinthians 13:8, in the New King James Version (NKJV), which sums it up perfectly, in just three words:

Love never fails.

The love that never fails is, of course, the unconditional love of God: agape.

What Is Agape, and How Does It Relate to the Presence of God?

As noted at the end of the preceding chapter, love is the greatest part of God's goodness, but it is so much more than that. Just as we did previously, let's first discuss what agape is not before we talk about what it is.

Agape is not a confused type of feeling that romantic love can bring. It is not a weird thought that occurs to a believer, nor does it have any boundaries or limits. It is not something

59

that humans can control or manipulate. It does not arrive from humans, only from God.

Let's repeat that to emphasize its importance: You can only receive agape from God. You can only receive it by His grace. We don't truly deserve it, but He gives it to us anyway. Because it comes from Him, we cannot control it.

Agape is the unconditional love of God. It is the love of God pouring into human flesh. And, yes, it has a lot to do with the presence of God: You cannot operate in the unconditional love (agape) of God unless the Holy Spirit pours it into you. Agape never fails. It believes in the best of everyone that it comes to contact with. Again, it is the divine unconditional love of God. When we love unconditionally, it is God's agape moving through our human flesh.

As Romans 5:5 tells us in the New King James Version (NKJV):

> Now hope does not disappoint, because the love of God has been poured out in our hearts by the Holy Spirit who was given to us.

Or, as the Good News Translation (GNT) phrases the same verse of Romans:

> We're not ashamed to have this confidence, because God's love has been poured into our hearts by the Holy Spirit, who has been given to us.

My Own Testimony

Several years ago, when the Holy Spirit first led me to start this ministry, I prayed to Him, asking, "What should we call this ministry? What is our purpose? What is it you want us to fulfill?"

He told me to call it Worldwide Agape Ministries. (We later abbreviated it as WAM.) Our ministry is filled with loving people, and the love flowing through us is the unconditional love of God. God commands us to love people with agape (His unconditional love). We demonstrate our love by loving people. Our mission is simply to love people into the kingdom of God. The love of God has truly opened up our hearts through loving people.

But let me back up to the beginning. Initially, when He first answered my question, my reaction, in prayer, was, "Lord! How do I do that?"

"By My Spirit," He said.

I could hear His voice within me, loud and clear.

He also told me, "You will do it by demonstrating My love to people; you are going to win lost souls for My kingdom."

Yes, by means of agape, all things are possible. Remember, agape is the supernatural love of God, flowing from Him to people in desperate need of His love.

Most people today are desperate, and so they seek love in all the wrong places—drugs, alcohol, and sex, for instance—but the truth is, none of these things can truly give us love. God is love. He does not just have love, but He *is* love. And He wants to give His love (agape) to you and to me.

As we read in 1 John 3:11 in the New King James Version (NKJV):

> For this is THE MESSAGE that you heard from the beginning that we should love one another.

And then, as we read further in 1 John 4:7–8 in the New King James Version (NKJV):

Beloved, let us love one another, for the love of God; for everyone who loves is born of God and knows God. He who does not love does not know God. For God is love.

His love came into my heart, and now it causes me to have compassion for those who have not allowed Jesus into their hearts. His presence will take effect when you accept Him and let him into your heart. It is truly the greatest gift anyone can hope for. But you only can receive this gift by your own choice.

God's love is pure. It is real. His love draws to people salvation. God's love is matchless; nothing can compare to it. And, remember, God does not just have love; He *is* love.

The world does not care how much you speak in tongues, although that is a very important gift to have. All the world cares about is seeing results. When agape is in you, it will be visible to everyone, and all the world will see the results.

It's true that the world doesn't really care about your great prophecies or your education. The world doesn't care about what you know. All people want to know is, What can you do for me? How can you help me? The answer is simple: agape.

How does your showing agape accomplish these things? Because you are demonstrating the love of God, that's how! Do so every day. For example, let's say that you know a young couple; they've been married for a few years, and they have some young children. They have not had an opportunity to go out with each other in a long while. Agape manifests in you, saying, "I'll watch the kids for you tonight. You two go out on a date."

The above example illustrates that agape is not only the love God shares with His people; it is also the answer to the problems we face today.

As Matthew 9:35–36 tells us in the New King James Version (NKJV):

> Then Jesus went about all the cities and villages, teaching in their synagogues, preaching the gospel of the kingdom, and healing every sickness and every disease among the people. But when He saw the multitudes, He was moved with compassion for them, because they were weary and scattered, like sheep having no shepherd.

The love of God gives you compassion for people. Agape touches the very core of your being. You may still wonder how agape relates to the presence of God. Well, agape has a great deal to do with the presence of God. Remember, God *is* love. And His love is the foundation of everything He does for us. Without that love, without agape, the power of God will not flow through or in you.

Let's look at another example from my own life. I went to the dentist to get some work done on my teeth. My wife went with me. While in the waiting room, I became impatient, feeling that we had been waiting a little too long. My impatience increased, and I soon became agitated. I wanted to leave, but I still needed dental care. Also, I knew I would never hear the end of it from my wife. Clearly, I needed to develop some patience in that area.

The following morning, we were exercising, and the topic of the dentist came up.

Jeanne said, "You need to develop some agape in that area."

I responded, "What does love have to do with it?"

She replied, under the anointing, "Everything has to do with love."

Jeanne was absolutely correct. Developing patience is positively a love walk.

My wife was operating under the anointing of the Holy Ghost, whereas I, through my impatience, was working completely in the flesh.

At that moment, I decided to hush; I did not bother to say another word until I got myself right.

As this example shows, when you operate in and with agape, it corrects you in all areas of your life, the weak areas as well as the great areas.

You might wonder why your boss is always on your case. It might just be that agape is working on your behalf, and you just don't know it yet. Perhaps you need correction in some area. God is attempting to get your attention in that area. You have to deal with whatever it is, and so God will keep prompting you until you get the message. You see, agape is always working to your benefit. Sometimes you may not even be aware of it. So, when uncomfortable situations like this arise, you must first confess that you have a weakness, and then you must deal with it; this is the only way to grow and become what God has intended for you and you alone. You want to get to the desired destination of point C, but you must go through points A and B. You will eventually get to point C, but there are no shortcuts. The truth is, God loves you very much. He does not want even one of His sons and daughters to be without Him. But you are the only one who can accept Him and His love and blessings.

God's love is already working for you. The blessing is on your life. The favor of God is on your life, which means the presence is there with you always. He said He will never leave you or forsake you. Why don't you rest in His presence?

In conclusion, enjoying the presence of the Lord every day simply means enjoying being in His presence. We must learn to include Him in our daily activities. If we are in the park, walking the dog, He is there. If we are exercising in the gym, He is there. He is wherever we are.

His presence is with you, wherever you are. He is in you, and you are in Him. The greater one resides in you. The way you receive that is by accepting Christ in your life.

One of the greatest gifts you can acquire is accepting Jesus Christ as your Lord and Savior. Once you make that decision, you will have eternal life. He will be with you always. You will never be alone; His presence will always be with you. (Read the "Prayer for Salvation and Baptism in the Holy Spirit," at the end of this book, and pray to receive Him as your Savior now, if you have not already done so.)

Accepting Jesus as your Savior is the greatest gift you can possibly receive. We read in Colossians 1:13–14 in the New King James Version (NKJV) that He has delivered us from the power of darkness and has translated us into the kingdom of His dear Son, in whom we have redemption through his blood, even the forgiveness of sin; that is His desire for all of us.

Yes, that is His desire for all of us. That is His agape.

Confession

Repeat these truths as often as you need to:

> I decree and declare that I have the agape of God working in me. It's in Him that I move and have my being. It is the hope and the glory. I have the joy of the Lord. The joy of the Lord is my strength. His agape continues to work in me all the days of my life.
>
> I have the anointing of God in me. I have the burden-removing, yoke-destroying, world-changing, devil-chasing, healing, delivering, explosive, supernatural, universe-creating power of the Holy Spirit flowing through me, enabling me to do what the flesh cannot do.
>
> In the mighty name of Jesus, amen.

Prayer for Salvation and Baptism in the Holy Spirit

Repeat these truths as often as you need to:

Heavenly Father, I come to You in the name of Jesus. The Bible tells us, "That whoever calls on the name of the Lord shall be saved" in the New King James Version of Acts 2:21. And so I am calling on You.

I pray and ask Jesus to come into my heart and be Lord over my life, according to Romans in the New King James Version (NKJV) of Acts: 10:9–10: "If I confess with my mouth the Lord Jesus and believe in my heart that God has raised Him from the dead, I shall be saved. For with the heart one believes unto salvation, and with the mouth confession is made unto salvation."

I do that now. I confess that Jesus is Lord, and I believe in my heart that God raised Him from the dead. I am a born-again child of God the Most High.

Father God, I am also asking You to fill me with the Holy Spirit. I receive You now, in the name of Jesus. The Holy Spirit rises up within me as I praise God. I fully expect to speak with other tongues, as You give me the utterance (Acts 2:4).

In the mighty name of Jesus, amen!

You can pray the above words as often as you need to and as often as you wish.

Begin to praise God for filling you with the Holy Spirit. Speak out the words and syllables you receive—not in your own language but in the language given to you by the Holy Spirit. Don't be concerned about what it sounds like. It is the heavenly language.

Pray in the Spirit (speak in tongues) every day in order to build yourself up spiritually. Also, spend time reading the Bible.

Find a good church that boldly preaches and teaches God's word, without compromise. Become part of a church family, where the people will love and care for you as you grow in the kingdom of God.

You are a born-again, Spirit-filled believer. You'll never be the same!